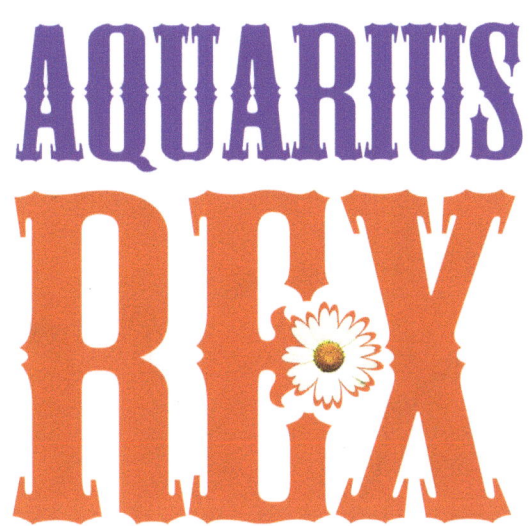

AQUARIUS REX

A PARABLE FOR OUR MODERN TIMES

Art and Words by

GORDY GRUNDY

PUBLISHERS
PLATFORM

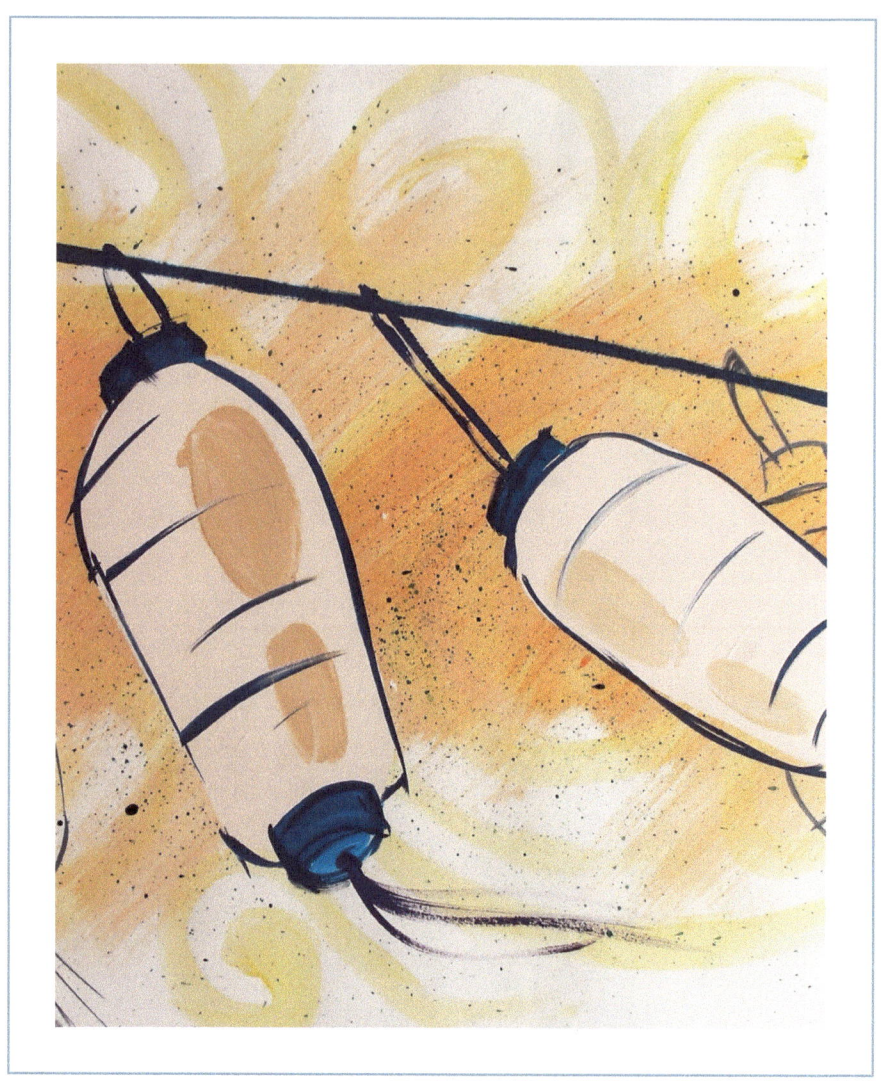

Detail, *Lanterns,* Painting on Paper

"The most beautiful experience we can have is the mysterious. It is the fundamental emotion, which stands at the cradle of true art and true science."

~ Al Einstein

"How little we know
How much to discover
What chemical forces flow
From lover to lover

How little we understand,
What touches off that tingle
That sudden explosion,
when two tingles intermingle

Who cares to define
What chemistry this is
Who cares with your lips on mine
How ignorant bliss is

So long as you kiss me,
And the world around us shatters,
How little it matters, how little know,
How little we know."

"How Little We Know"
~ Frank Sinatra, Carolyn Leigh,
Phillip Springer

AQUARIUS REX

Words and Images Copyright © 2016 Gordy Grundy

2016 Gordy Grundy Press Trade Paperback Edition

All Rights Reserved.

Published in the United States of America

ISBN-13: 978-0692664599 (Gordy Grundy)
ISBN-10: 0692664599

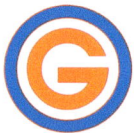

www.GordyGrundy.com

PUBLISHERS
PLATFORM

AQUARIUS
REX

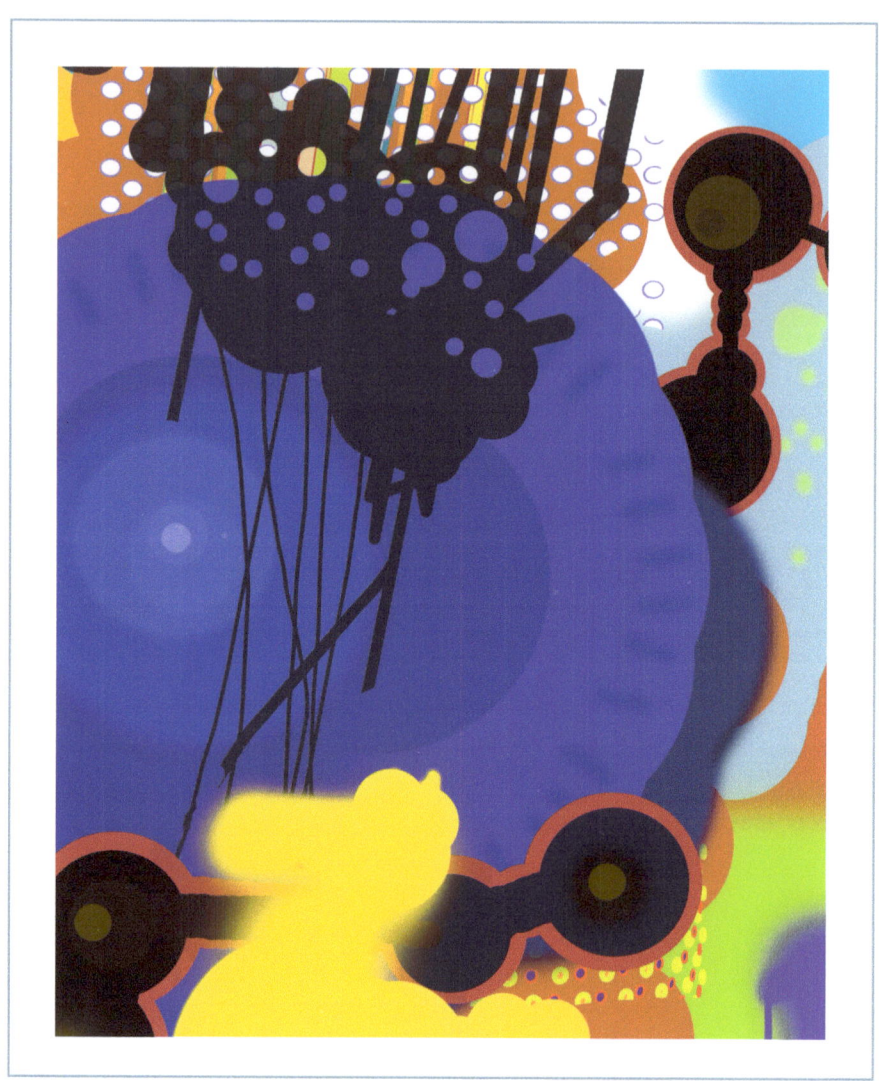

Detail, *Aquarius Rex No. 34,* Mixed Media

THE BONFIRE snapped and popped. A log fell onto another and bright ember sparks flew up into the clear night sky and got lost between a million stars.

"It's funny, and true, when they say that the world can stop on a dime. Even when the world was ending, she stopped on a dime. The old girl careened into a wildly flying and graceful stop. Just when things were as bad as they ever could be, it flipped on a dime. *Life...*

"Everyone left standing aboard planet Earth was shaken to their core. Who would have thought? *Everyone was surprised.* That was the greatest gift of all, to be surprised.

"Everyone had become so jaded, no one thought they would ever, *could ever*, be surprised again. And they were. We all were. Aquarius Rex surprised us all.

"In the turmoil, we had taken *surprise* for granted. Everyone was so bombarded by radical creatures, earthly upheavals and ungodly tragedies that we failed to notice the daisies.

"Like the flying monkeys, the she-wolves and the rest, the daisies suddenly appeared and began to rain from the sky.

"White daisies, with bright orange centers, softly, happily, drifted down from the sky, like a lazy rain.

"Everywhere, daisies.

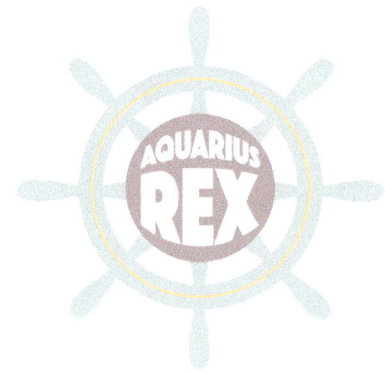

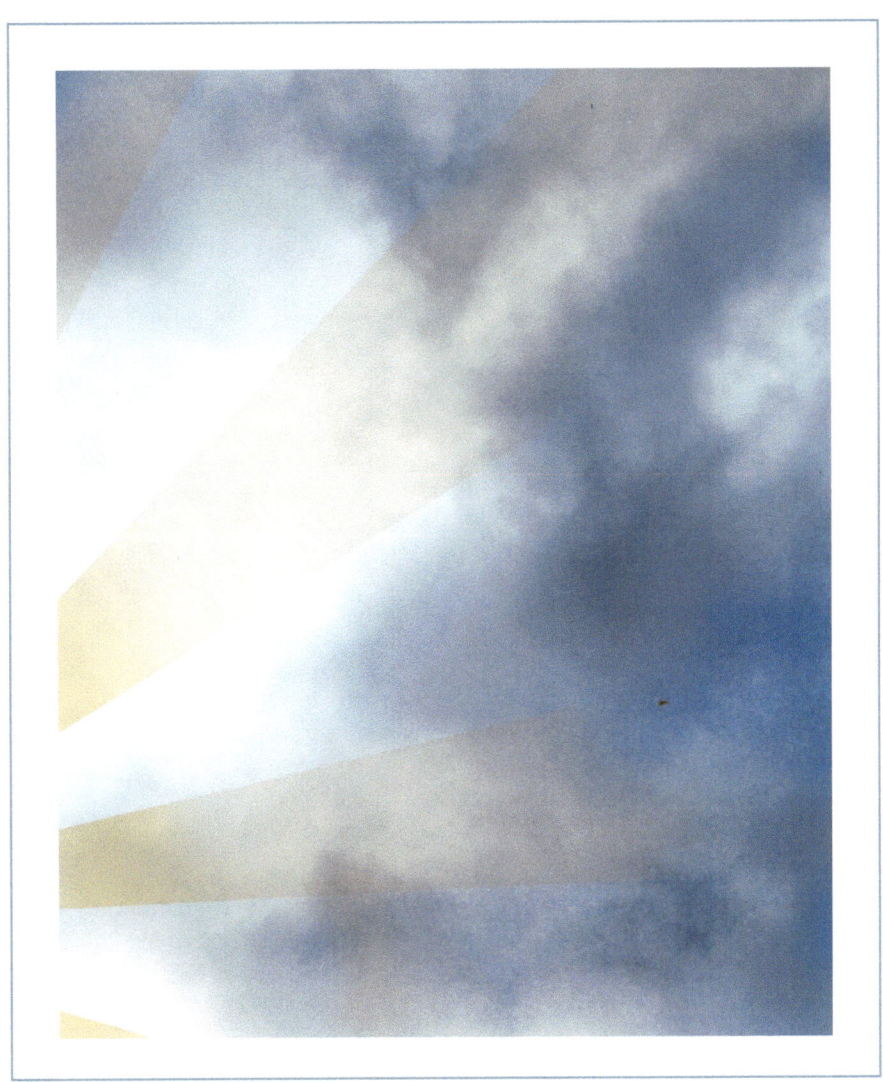

Detail, *Aquarius Rex No. 11*, Mixed Media

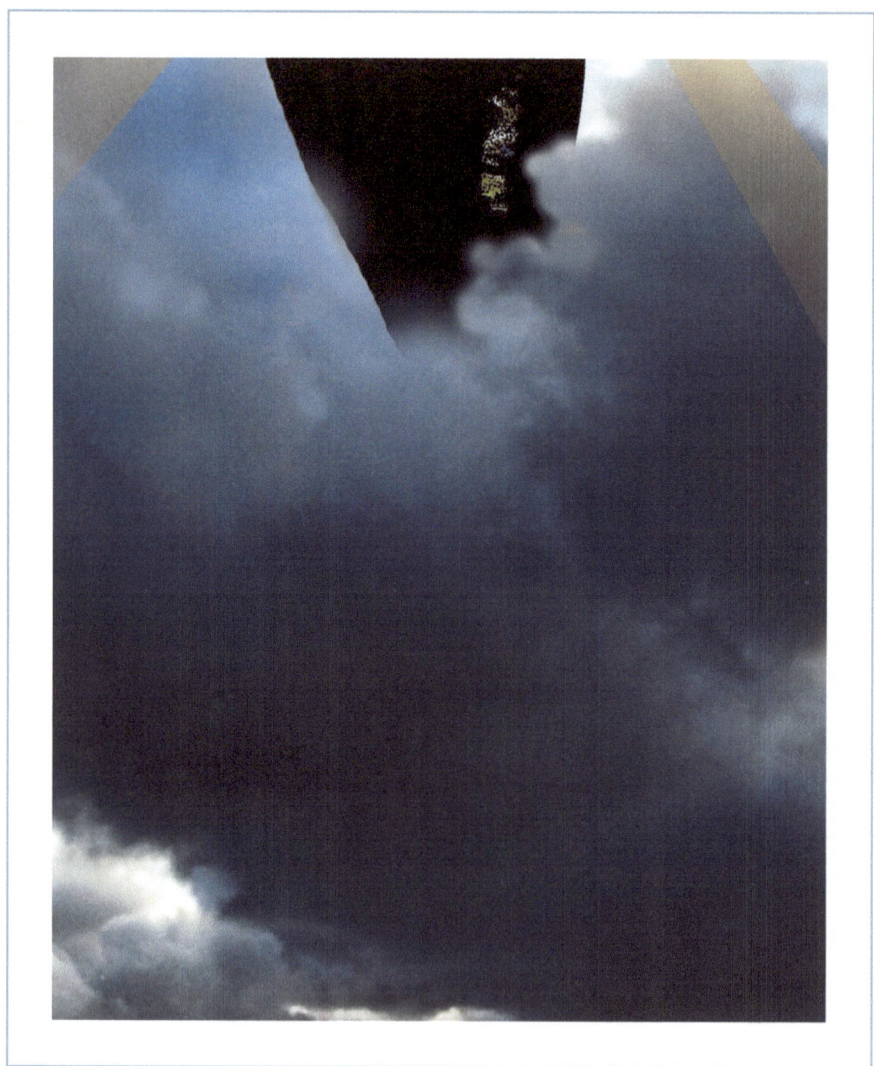

Detail, *Aquarius Rex No. 9,* Mixed Media

"SOME SAY the End of the World began on the day she was born. Like any pulsing life, we live through the many moments, large and small, until there are no more.

"One can best argue that the End of the World began with the internet and the handheld device. This lifestyle-changing phenomena that promised so much, became, in the end, a source of much destruction. Industries, jobs, professions and dignities were slowly obliterated. In the end, the internet was a success for only a small handful of people.

"The social evils had little consequence in the end. Privacy, digital humanity, cyber-lovemaking and social community no longer mattered after the fifth electromagnetic explosion.

"Soon, everyone went back to tin soup cans and taunt string.

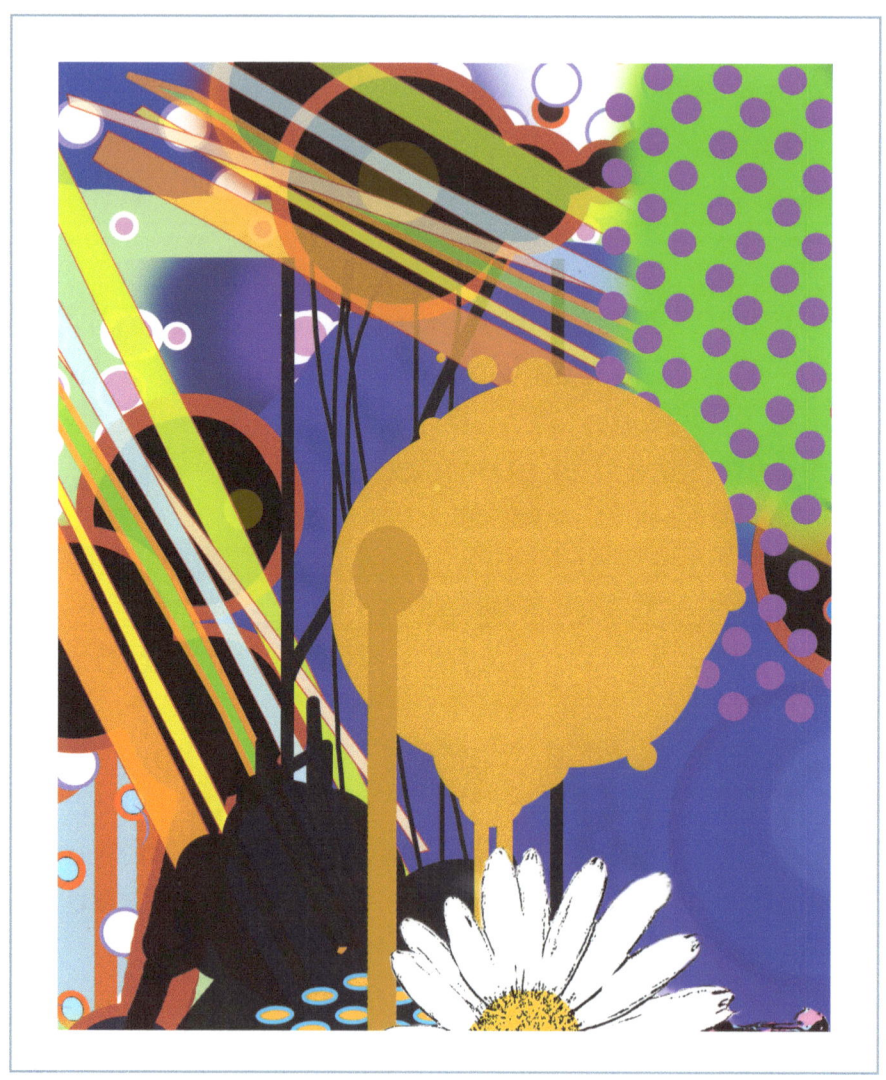

Detail, *Aquarius Rex No. 32,* Mixed Media

"THE APOCALYPSE or the End of the World As We Know It *came to pass*, pretty much, *as hath been written*. Most of the old religious prophesies materialized in some manner. From the Bible to the Koran to a Jehovah Witness newsletter, it all generally happened in spectacularly visual and symphonic ways. The pestilence, wars and nature's stunning chaos followed an unauthored script.

"Every one ignored all of the warning signs on the Drudge Report. The world was littered with unholy cloud formations, birds falling, weather exploding, bees dying, madmen shouting, lights in the sky and murderers amassing. We were so preoccupied we couldn't see it coming.

"The epidemics of dis-ease read like a ghoulish laundry list. Before one plague could vanish, another delivered a new, fresh horror. These evils took hundreds of millions of lives and then stole more.

"At this time, much evidence was unfolding, proof that mankind's efforts to enhance, genetically modify or control Nature had backfired in every way. Zika was the first disease that bent humankind in half, weeping, "What have we wrought? *How arrogant we were!* How little we knew!"

"Best intentions" was the gross *mea culpa*.

"As mankind sought to earn his bloodthirsty reputation, Mother Nature responded with a roar in a demonstration of sheer power. Volcanic eruptions and earthquakes detonated daily. The Pacific was a Ring of Fire. The oceans inhaled and exhaled with force. Winds sandpapered cities and tsunamis washed them away.

"In the dry desert, all of the world's forces gathered where the crescent was no longer fertile. A pie chart of international alliances, both economic and political, looked like an abstract expressionist painting.

"A misprint on a work order started it all, the nuclear reprisals. It was the accident everyone had been waiting for. Insult upon injury and buttons were pushed. Arsenals were emptied. Hell broke loose, all around.

"It became a blur of tragedy, manmade and naturally caused. One could not remember every Los Angeles bombing, Brazilian tsunami or Mediterranean eruption. It was too close, too much, all the time.

"As ugly as it all was, there was great beauty. The visions were magnificent, colorful, breathtaking and otherworldly.

"This attitude became a mantra common among the survivors. *"For Beauty! To live for Beauty!"* we all cried.

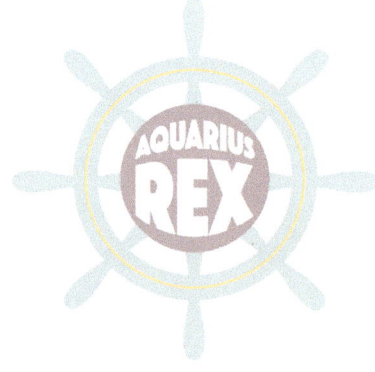

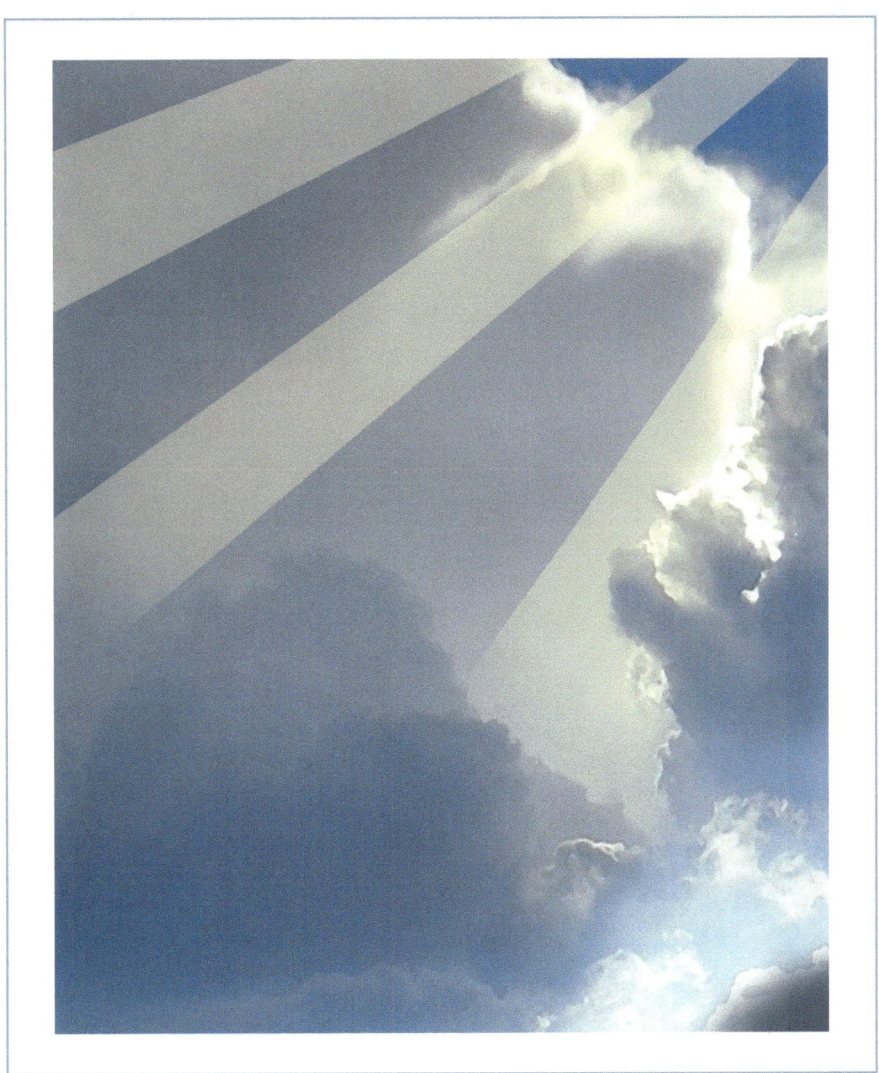

Detail, *Aquarius Rex No. 11*, Mixed Media

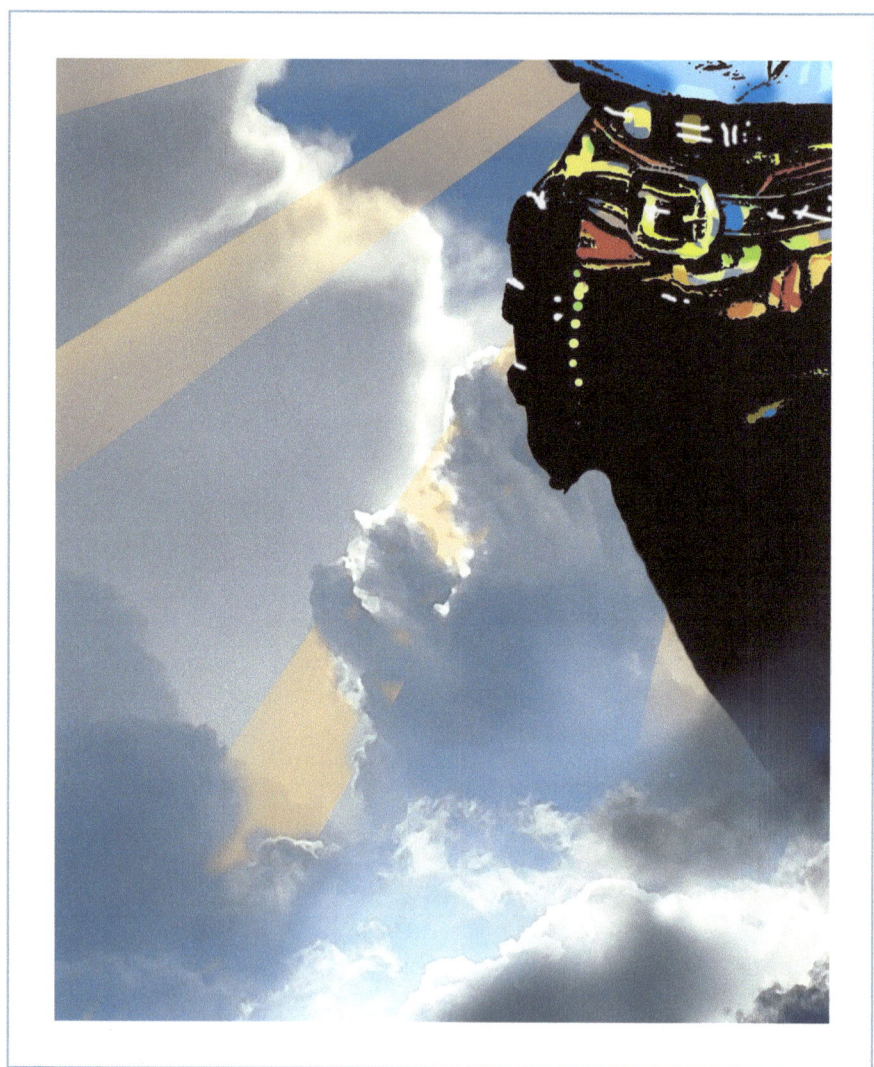

Detail, *Aquarius Rex No. 44*, Mixed Media

"EARLY ON, a third of the world's population vanished, mysteriously, overnight. They were of every race, creed and sex. Young and old, poor and rich, beautiful and ugly, couth and unmannered, they all vanished together. Religion was not a factor. 2.4 billion people vanished. That was another world event.

"Speculation was rife. Everyone wanted to know their secret. Everyone was hoping to ascend the hell outta here. A cottage industry was born. As best as anyone could gather, those who vanished were genuine, honest, responsible types that got things done.

"After this ascension, governments slowly ceased to function. Skilled workers had vanished. Suppliers no longer served. Businesses were leaderless. Bad decisions were made.

"Everything broke down.

"Survival is a tough business.

"The OneWorld Government grew out of greed and opportunity, not practicality.

"Humanity was fighting on many levels. Every day brought a new epic of biblical proportions. Another major city vanished and loves were lost.

"There was no safety, no place to hide. The constant fear and fret, the worry killed more people than the warfare. For so long, people had been cocooning their lives, distancing themselves from reality and self. Rather quickly, every one was stripped bare. Many died of their emotional nakedness.

"The battlefield stunk. It stank of testosterone and estrogen, overheated and sweating angry, human, animal and the new breeds, the genetic mutations. Everyone fought for everything.

"And it came to pass. All of the players were in position. The New World leaders circled, blustered and shook their angry fists.

"Because so many interesting and surprising things were going on, no one noticed the daisies that began to float down from the sky.

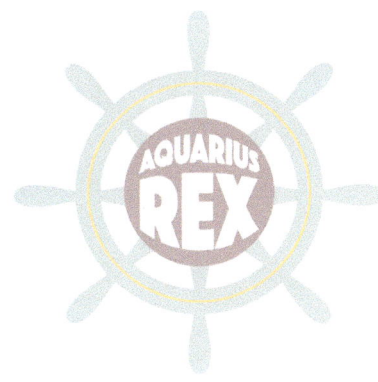

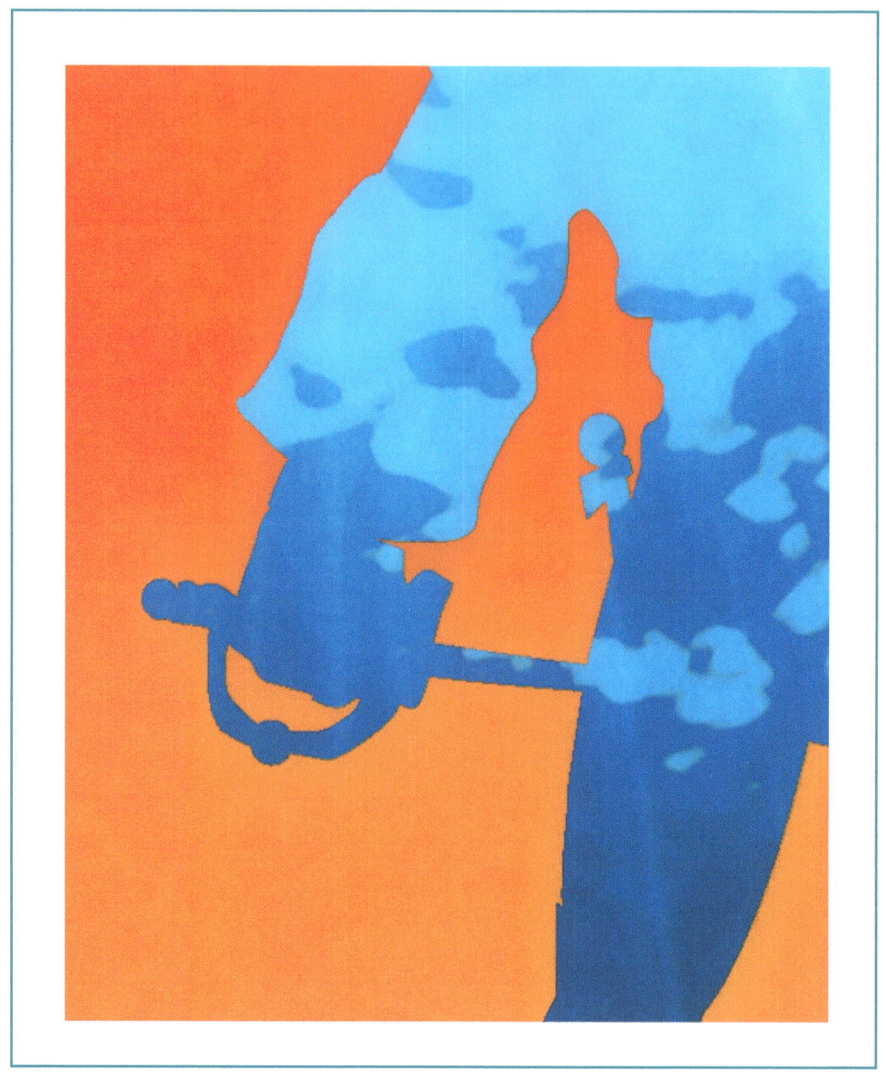

Detail, *Buccaneer*, Mixed Media

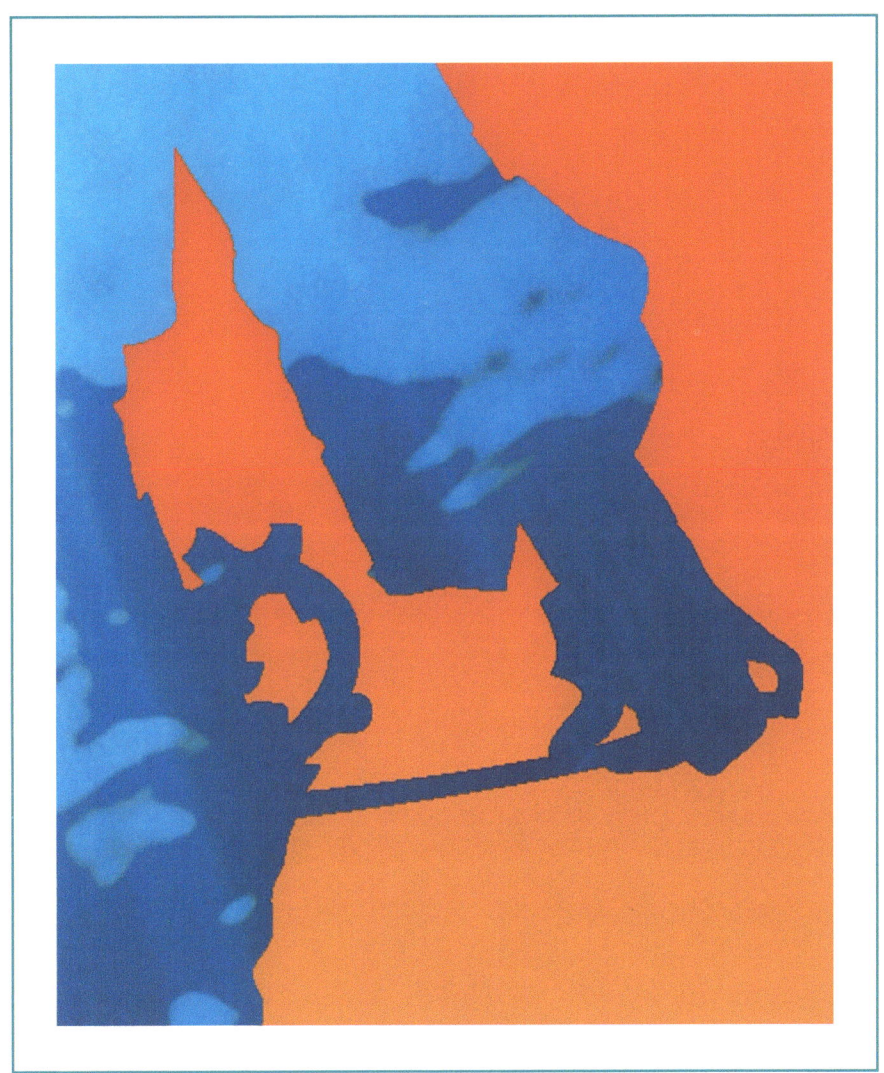

Detail, *Buccaneer,* Mixed Media

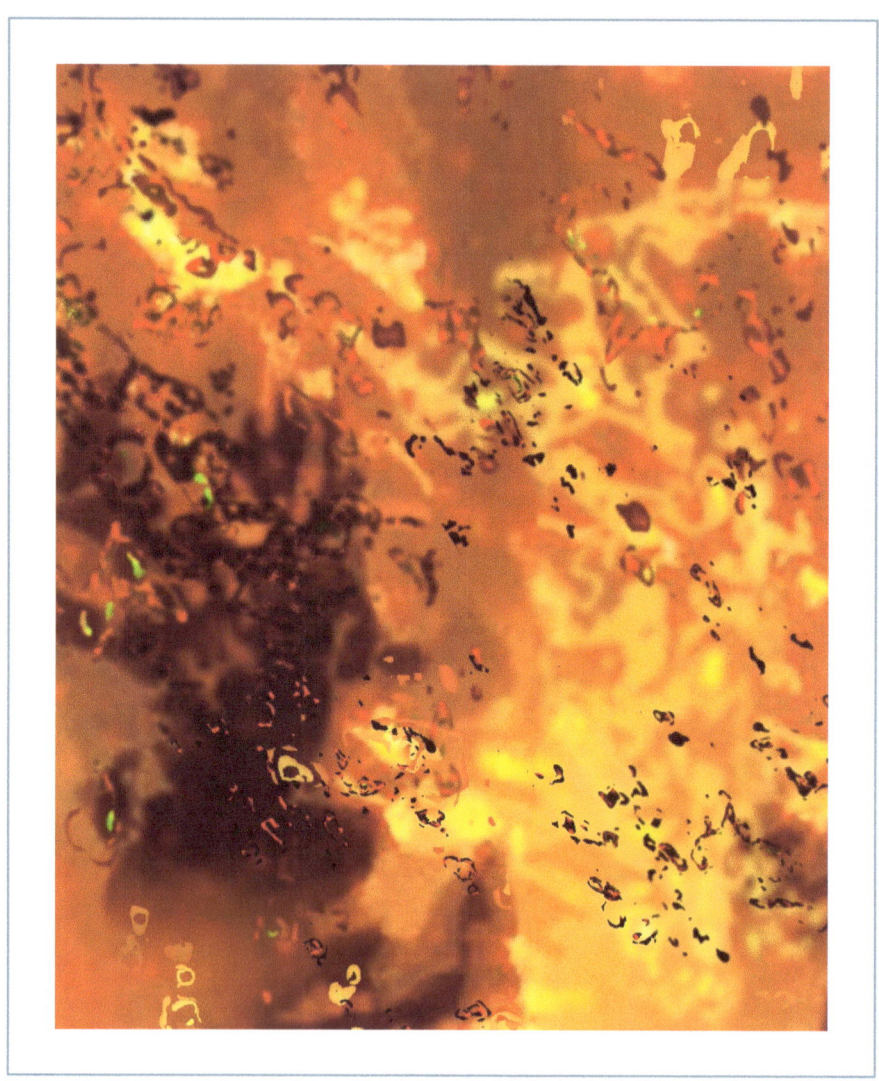

Detail, *Apocalypse Rex No. 13,* Mixed Media

"AS THE ARMIES of the world converged on Dabiq and Jerusalem, those at the head table were modified with incredible powers. Remember, by this time, there were no surprises anymore. Everyone had just about seen everything. So when the Mahdi, Jesus Christ, Isa the Islamic Jesus, the Trimurti, the Maitreya and the Antichrist grew to giant size in a beat down, it wasn't that big of a deal. It was expected actually.

"The War of the Gargantuans was violent and ugly. The impassioned armies fought viciously. The Mahdi had the Antichrist in a headlock; both were as tall as skyscrapers. Isa was uniting Islam in blood and wielding the Eiffel Tower as a cudgel. Knocked from his floating golden throne,

Jesus Christ fired a light beam at the Antichrist and severed her arm at the elbow.

"Suddenly a big man, as tall as the sun, sprinted up quickly. His appearance surprised everyone. He was a cowboy in a dusty Stetson hat. Charging hard with outstretched arms, Aquarius Rex caught their heads and knocked them together.

"The great powers of the east, west and the heavens had their heads klonked together. The sound was heard worldwide. It sounded like bonking coconuts.

"Concussed, the Gods all fell into a dizzy pile.

"Aquarius Rex reached down and tousled their hair, as if small children. "Y'all gonna get along now.""

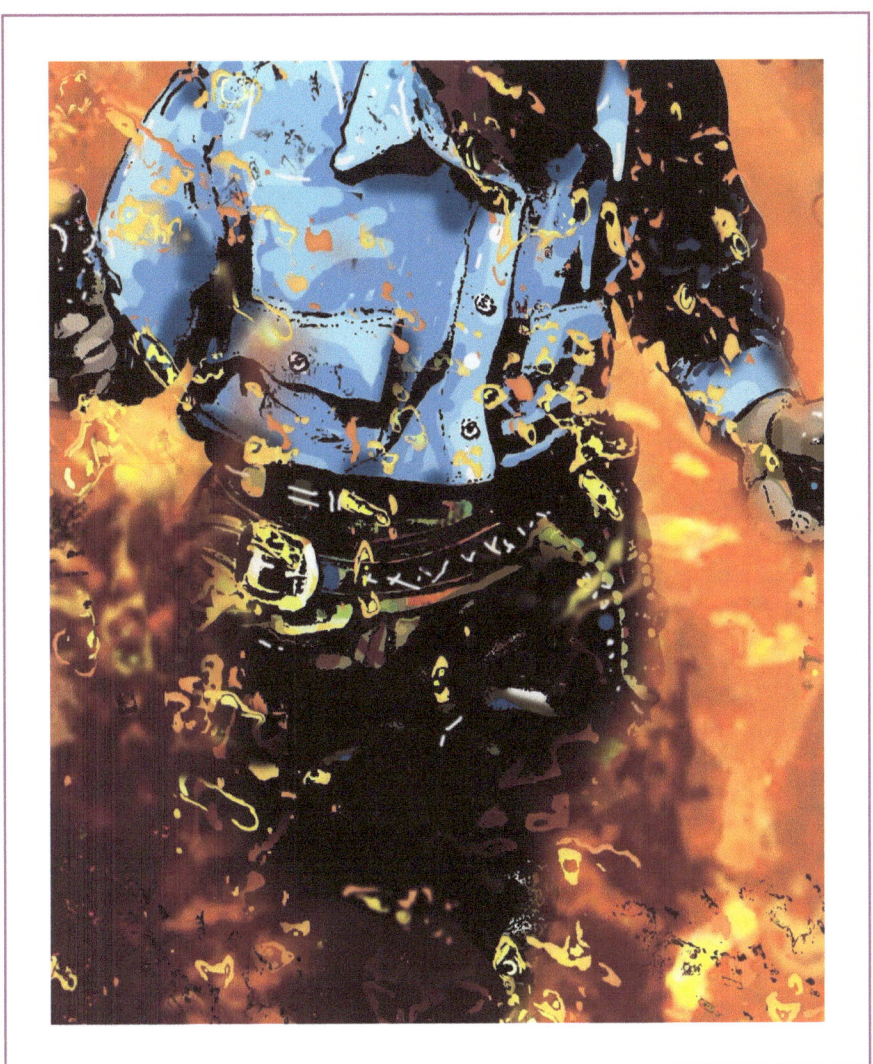

Detail, *Aquarius Rex No. 76,* Mixed Media

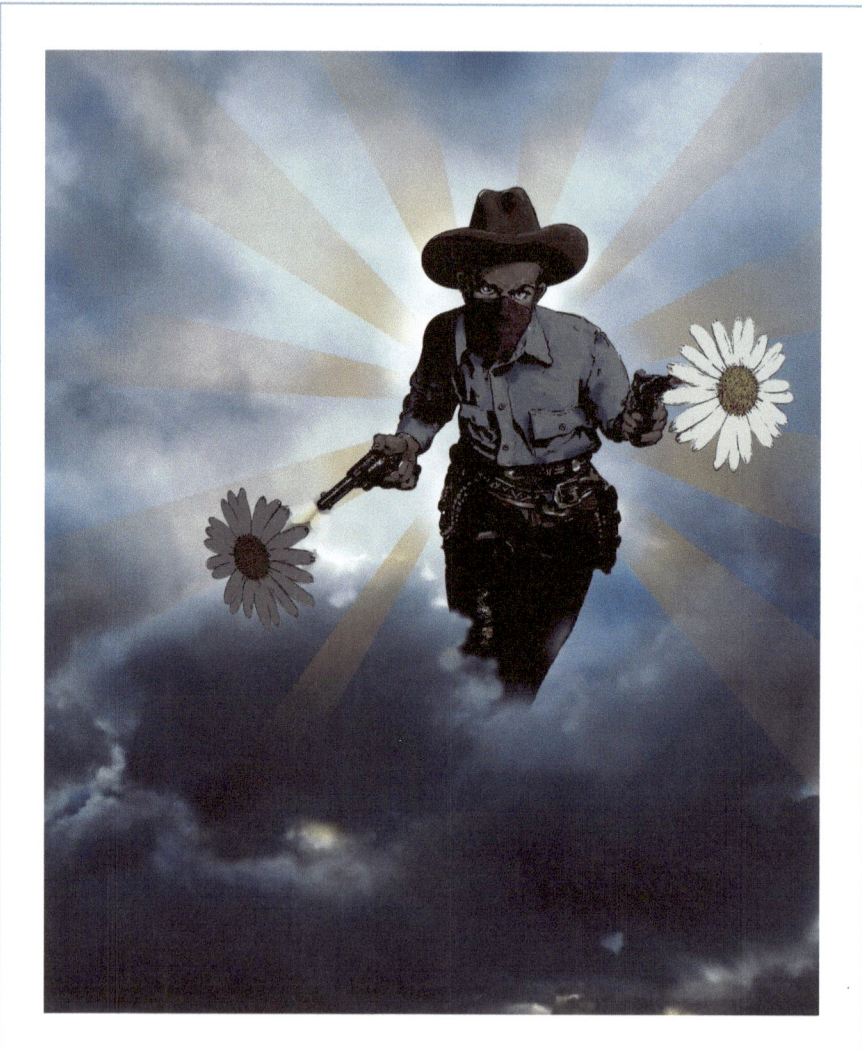

Detail, *Aquarius Rex No. 69*, Mixed Media

"AQUARIUS REX grew ever taller. The top of his hat touched the stratosphere. His cowboy shirt matched the color of the sky. He shifted and placed his massive left boot squarely onto the Vatican, demolishing Rome. His legs straddled the Mediterranean. Then, he settled his right boot deep in Mecca. And there he stood for forty days. His arms were loosely crossed against his chest and there was a smile on his face.

"The giant paniolo cast a long shadow across the world.

"In that short time, a dense forest of redwood trees grew for hundreds of miles around his boots. It happened so fast. Most of the redwoods grew to three hundred feet in forty days. Rome and Saudi Arabia became overgrown woodlands and quiet, green idylls.

"Aquarius Rex laughed. With lightening speed, he crouched low, drew his pistols and fired twelve shots. Boom. Boom. Boom. Twelve giant daisies flew from his flaming silver pistols and burst into thousands more. A breathtaking bombardment of Love. Daisies rained from the sky and everyone was delighted and surprised.

"Rex blew the smoke from the barrel of each pistol. "Lotsa shots-a love!" he exclaimed.

"He holstered the spinning pistols into his braided leather belt and tucked his thumbs inside the front pocket of his jeans. He winked and said, "Lotsa shots-a love."

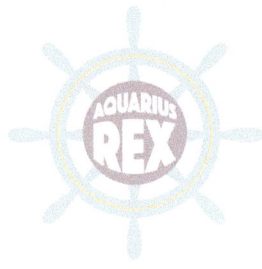

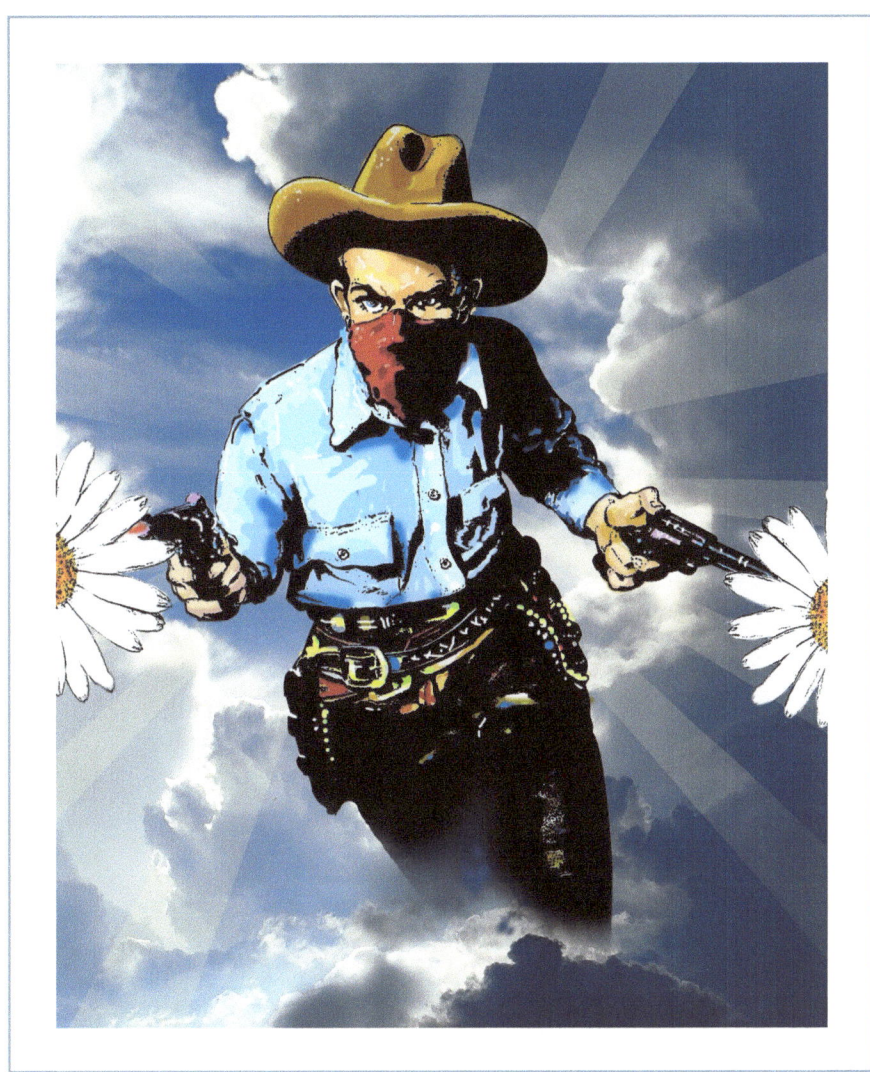

Detail, *Aquarius Rex No. 7*, Mixed Media

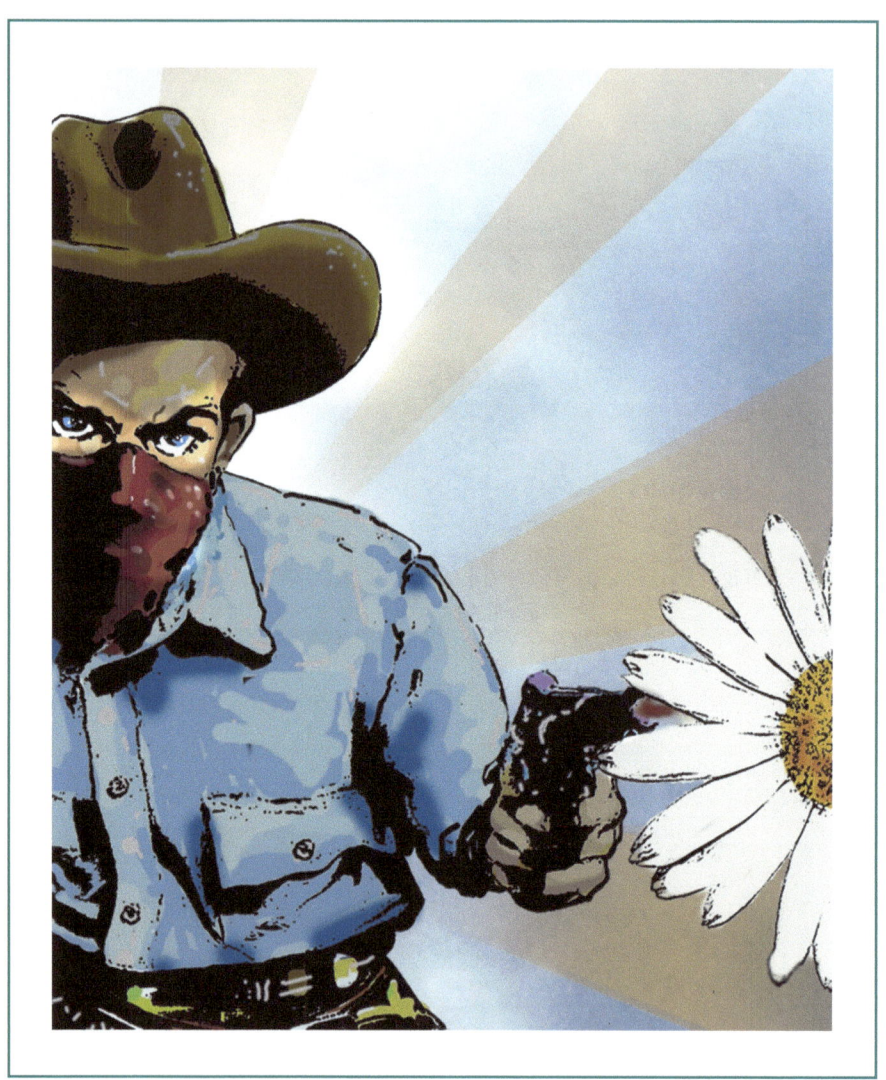

Detail, *Aquarius Rex No. 27,* Mixed Media

"AQUARIUS REX never got mad, just patiently humored and a bit buggered. It didn't happen often, but Rex would get hot at an injustice. He is a spitfire whenever anyone sought to enslave another; mankind has developed so many clever ways. Simply, he would grow as tall as a mountain, poke a long finger at the horror and a forest of California redwoods would suddenly grow tall in its place. Rex created quite a few forests. Most of them used to be the capitals of the world.

"Aquarius Rex took a deep breath and blew a mighty wind. Across the globe, the smoke from the fires and the cloudy toxins were cleared from the skies. Everyone looked up with awe into the fresh, new blue.

"When standing tall, Aquarius Rex could cross an ocean with a casual step. Most often, Rex roamed the land as a common man of common size. "Take care of yourself. And then, help your brother." Rex was always eager to lend his strong back. He was quick to roll up his sleeves and dig in.

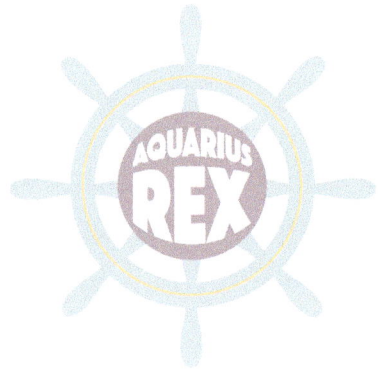

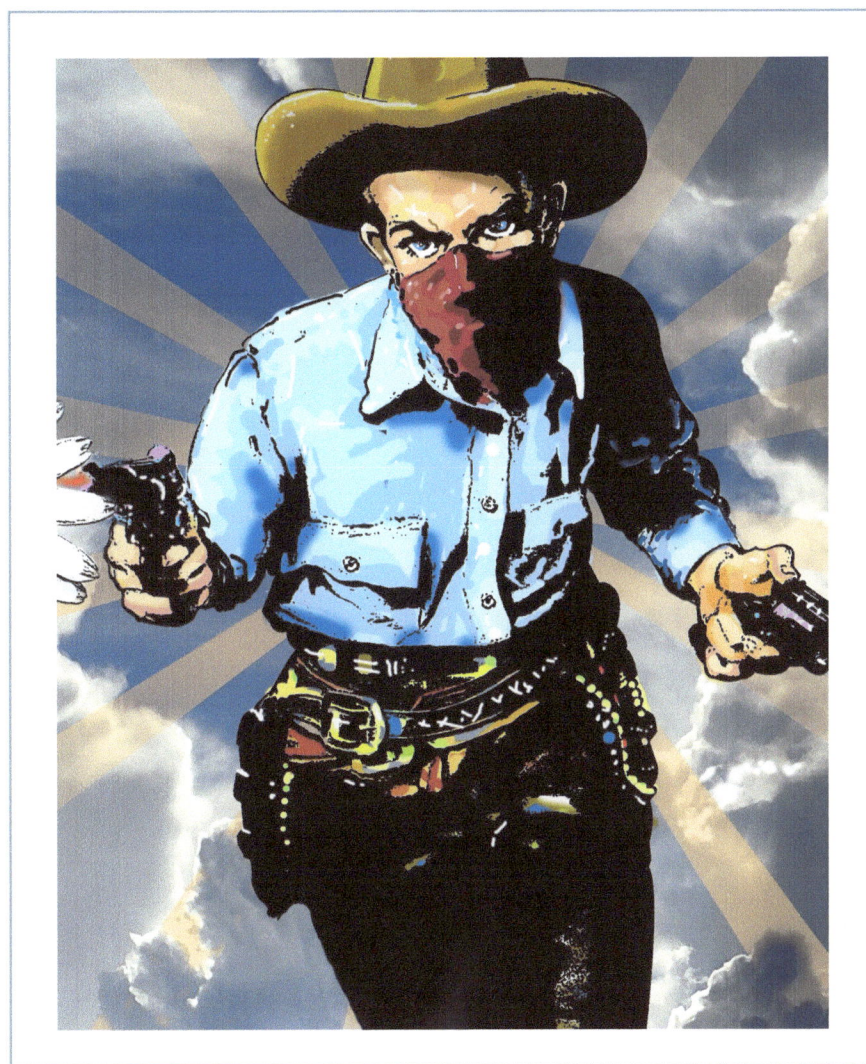

Detail, *Aquarius Rex No. 13*, Mixed Media

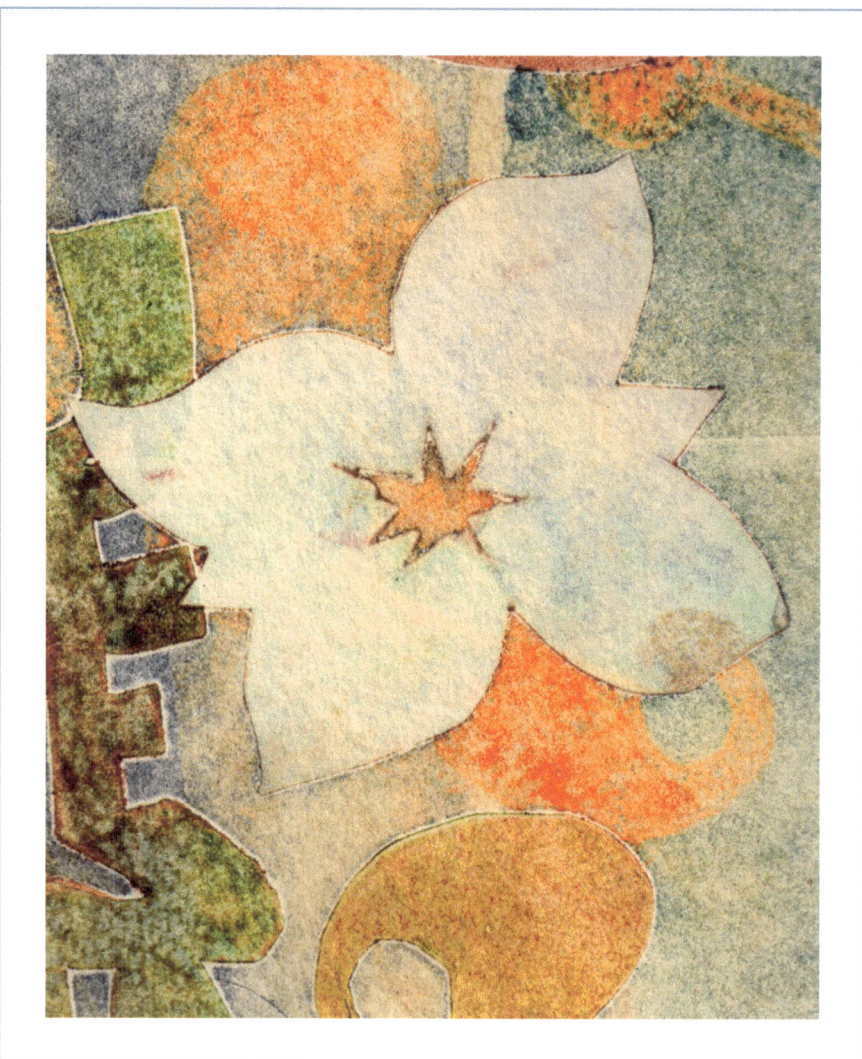

Detail, *TikiFlower Aquarius,* Monoprint

"THE EARTH had stopped convulsing. Soon Gaia, at Pele's core, was busy humming and waltzing, in a new, faster twirl on the celestial dance floor. Everyone could feel the energy and the vibration in the ground beneath your feet. Like all living things, the earth was growing and decaying and very much alive.

"An appreciation for Beauty became the highest value and reward.

"His visits were met with great celebration. Laughing and dancing are the greatest expressions of love and joy and Rex is always quick to initiate both. With a wide smile, Rex would always crow, "Laughter oxygenates your soul!"

"The Vanished returned. Not one could remember where they had been. They paid the missing past no mind. Their focus was on the present. With joy, zeal and great industry, they sought to feather their new nests.

"It felt like waking up from a nap, stretching, warm in the afternoon sun. The sound of the waves rolling against the beach was steady and hushed.

"The Apocalypse had been stressful and savage. People had forgotten how to feel and breathe. They let the sun shine in.

"Suddenly, the soul was no longer paralyzed and enslaved. Everyone opened their arms, shrugged their shoulders and sighed deeply.

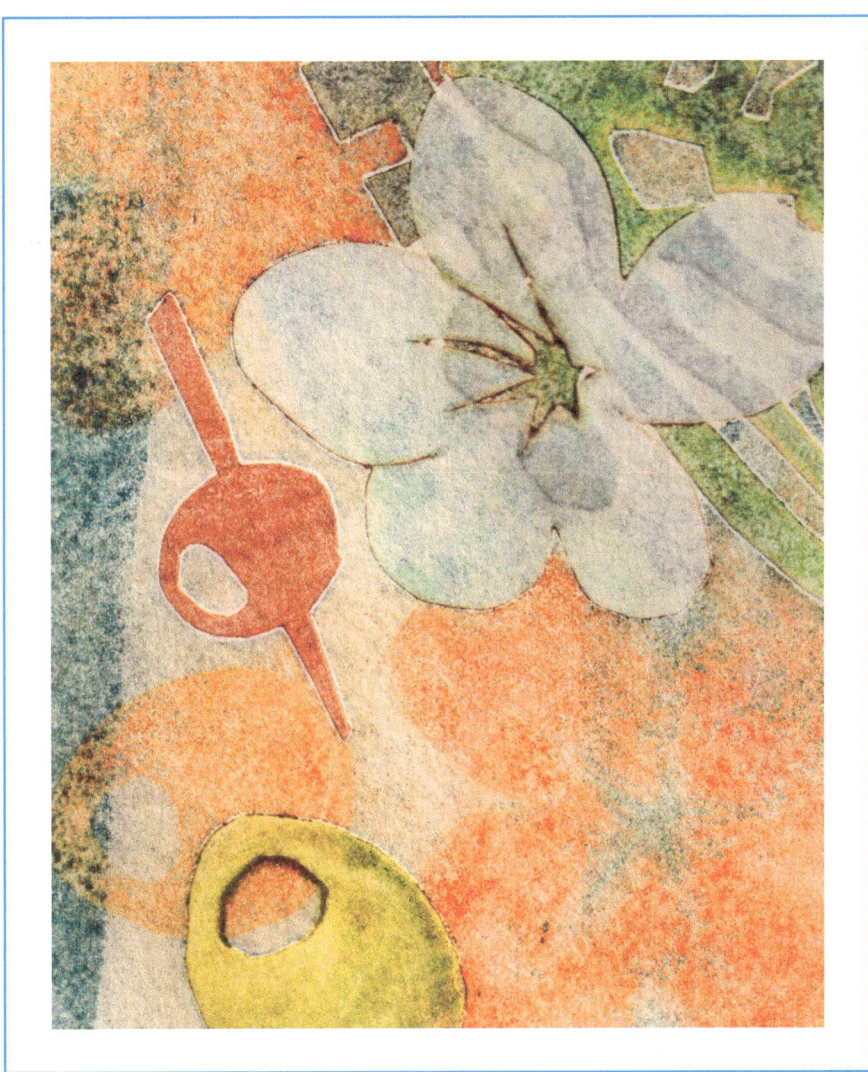

Detail, *TikiFlower Twilight*, Monoprint

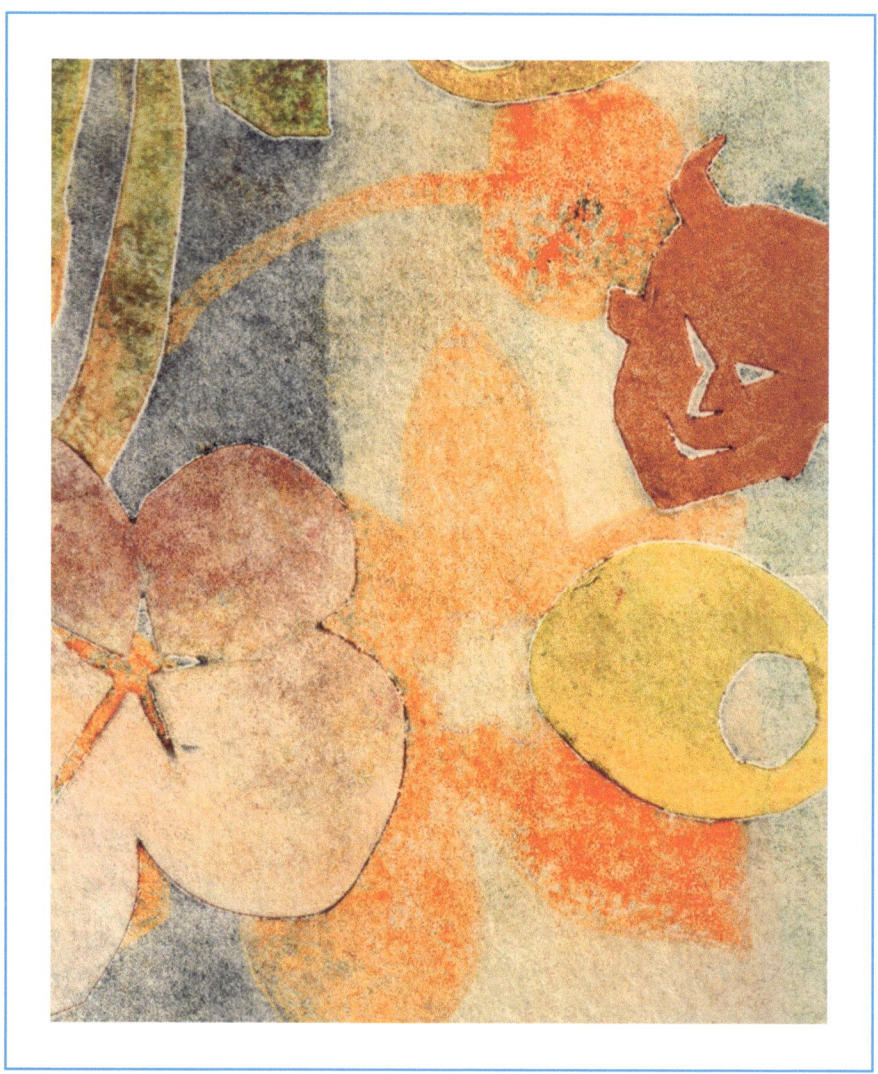

Detail, *TikiFlower*, Monoprint

"MANKIND GREW FOND of

itself once again. People needed each other to trade services, shelter and food. Fair markets and communities grew and prospered organically. People made what they needed and nothing more. There was harmony, understanding and freedom. Reason and Love fueled peace, sensibility and all good things.

"Many tried to praise Rex as a god and a deity. Always, he would laugh. "*Pshaw!* You know everything you need to know! Be quiet and look inside! Y'all don't need *me*." At that point, he would usually strap his guitar behind his back and hightail it to another town.

"When he was feeling transcendent or tickled pink, Aquarius Rex would grow to a starry height and laugh, a big booming whoop. The lively echo would bounce around the world. Most of the people and all the animals would start laughing, for laughter is infectious.

"Aquarius Rex said, "I always try to be *better than*. Everyday, I will leave everywhere I go, better than I found it. I want to leave everyone I meet, better for the encounter."

"This is the new Age of Aquarius."

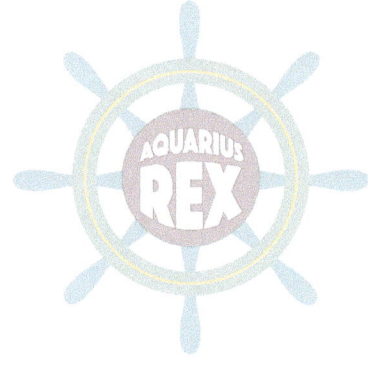

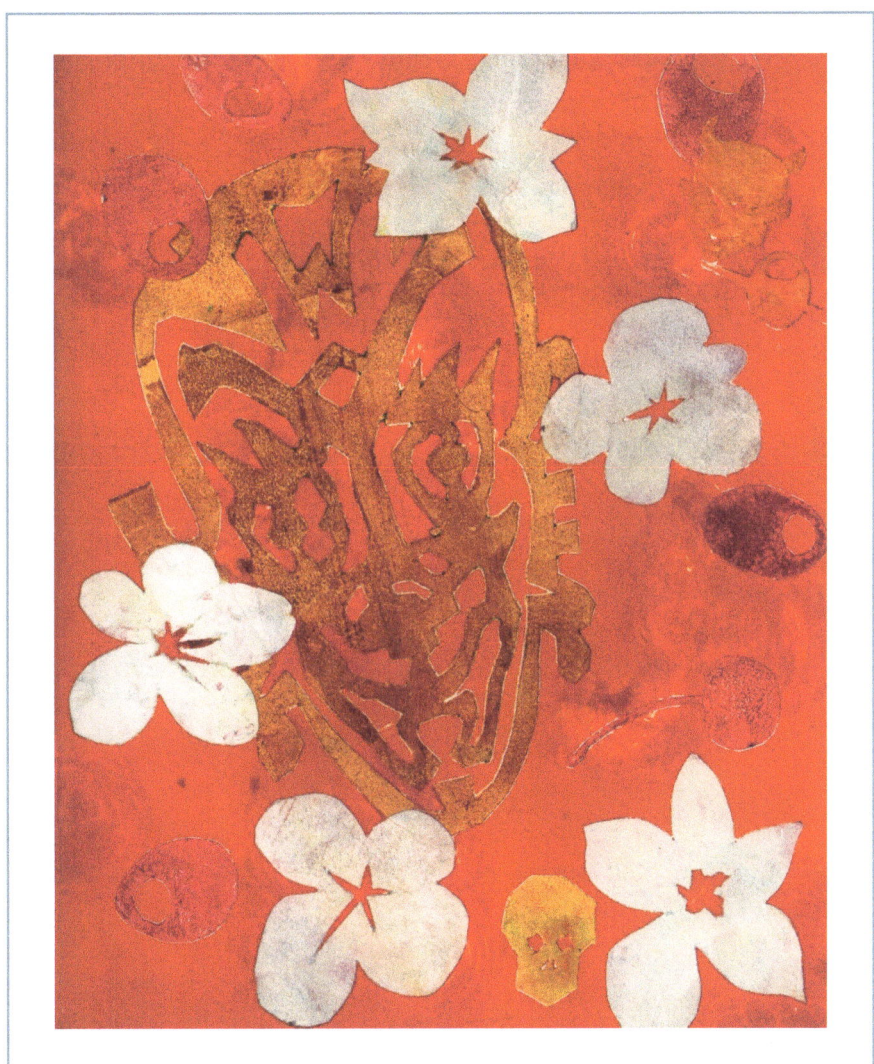

Detail, *Tiki Aquarius, No. 21,* Monoprint

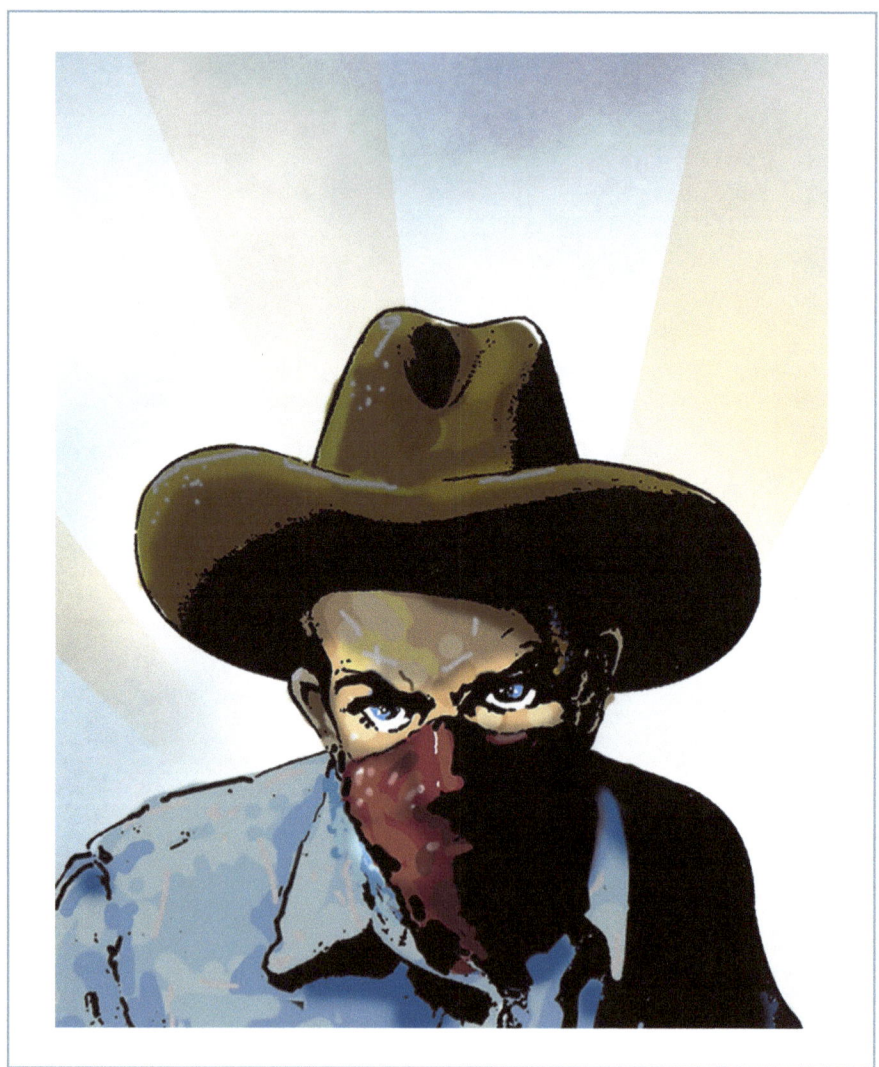

Detail, *Aquarius Rex, No. 33*

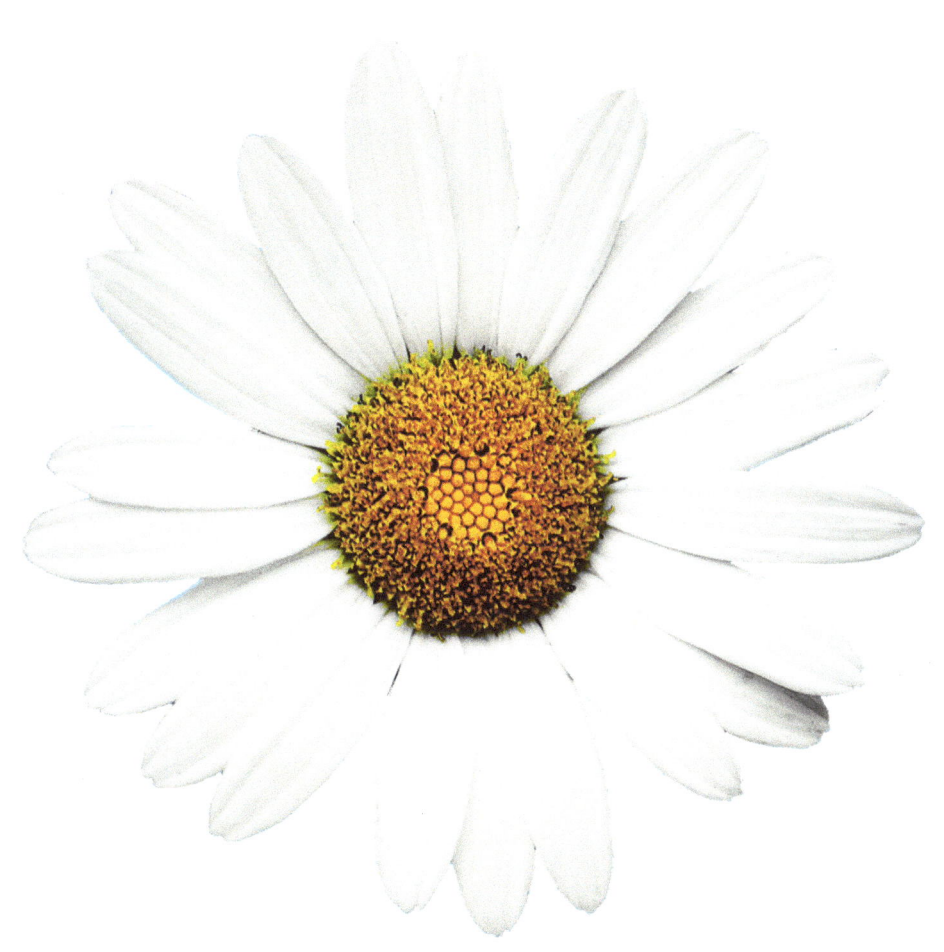

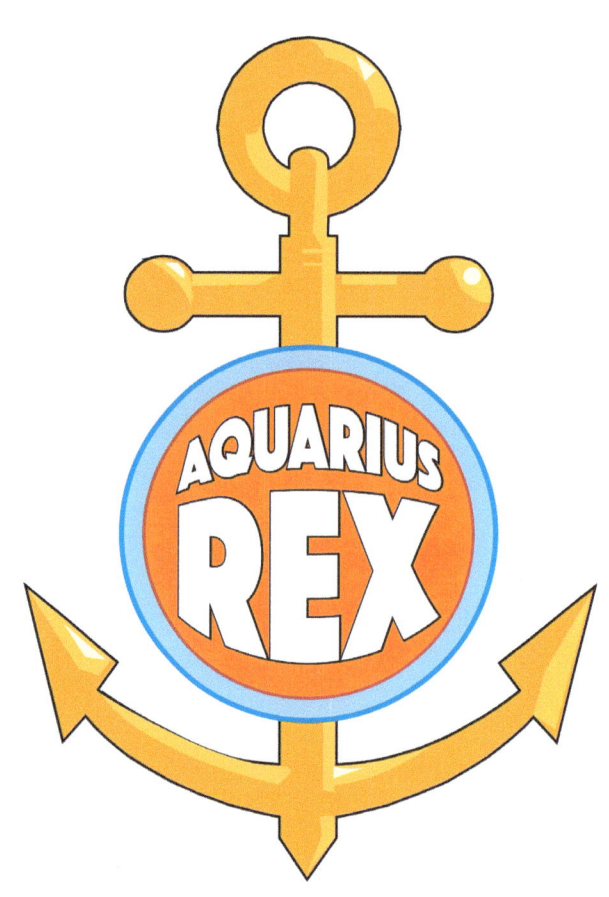

GORDY GRUNDY is an American artist and arts writer. He has been influenced by sunny flights of SoCal fancy, lost causes, the bold stroke and the beautiful gesture.

The Southern California sensibility has always been his touchstone. Light & Space, Minimalism, Hollywood, Disney, the secrets of re-creation and the Healing Power of Pop continue to fascinate him.

As a writer and columnist, he has written for *Artillery Magazine, the Huffington Post, the Los Angeles Times, the LA Weekly, ArtNews, the Coagula Art Journal* and many others.

His favorite creation *No Further West,* a gold leaf, minimalist painting, hangs at Traxx Restaurant in Union Station, Los Angeles.

His visual and literary works can be found at www.GordyGrundy.com

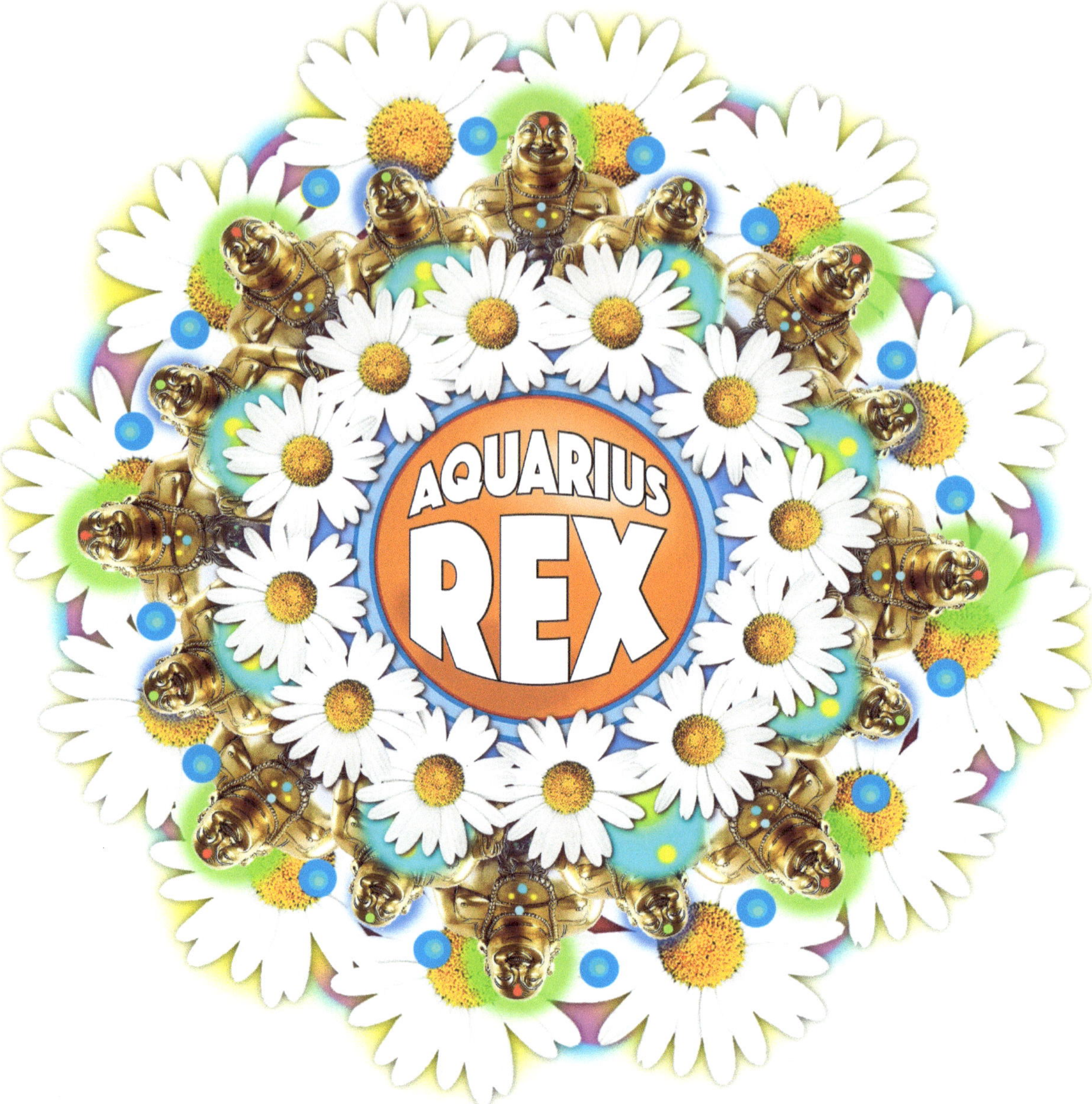

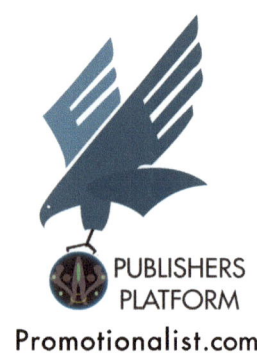

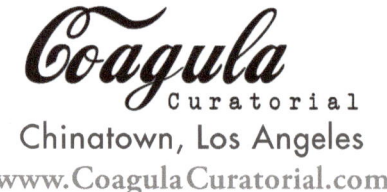